Newbridge Discovery Links®

The Body in Motion

Lisa Trumbauer

D0731237

Newbridge

A Haights Cross Communications ✕ Company

The Body in Motion
ISBN: 1-58273-722-3

Program Author: Dr. Brenda Parkes, Literacy Expert
Content Reviewer: Christine Hopple, Instructor,
  Health Promotion & Human Movement, Ithaca College, Ithaca, NY
Teacher Reviewer: Sherri Strating, Horace Mann Lab School,
  Northwest Missouri State University, Maryville, MO

Written by Lisa Trumbauer
Editorial and Design Assistance by Curriculum Concepts

Newbridge Educational Publishing
333 East 38th Street, New York, NY 10016
www.newbridgeonline.com

Cover Photograph: Basketball players in action
Table of Contents Photograph: Children competing in a footrace

Photo Credits
Cover: Alvis Upitis/The Image Bank; Contents page: Lawrence Migdale/Stock Boston; page 4: Jim
Cummins/The Stock Market; page 5: Bob Daemmrich/Stock Boston; page 6: Lawrence Migdale/Stock
Boston; page 7: Mug Shots/The Stock Market; page 9: Adam Petty/Allsport USA; pages 10–11: Don
Mason/The Stock Market; page 13: (top) David Woo/Stock Boston, (bottom) David Stoecklein/The Stock
Market; page 14: Jose Pelaez/The Stock Market; page 15: Roy Morsch/The Stock Market; page 16: Bob
Daemmrich/Stock Boston; page 17: John Weizanbach/The Stock Market; page 19: (left & right) Todd
Warchaw/Allsport USA; page 21: Michael Kevin Daly/The Stock Market; page 22: Craig Jones/Allsport
USA; page 23: William Sallaz/Duomo/CORBIS; pages 24–25: Craig Jones/Allsport USA; page 26: Doug
Peninger/Allsport USA; page 30: Larry Williams/The Stock Market

Illustrations on pages 8, 12, 18, 20, 26, 28–29 by Barb Cousins

10 9 8 7 6 5 4 3

Table of Contents

Built to Move

Every season, people marvel at the amazing feats that athletes accomplish. Soccer players show dazzling footwork as they maneuver the ball up and down the field. Basketball players catch and pass the ball, dribble it down the court, and slam it into the basket. And pole-vaulters fearlessly soar high against the sky, up and over the bar.

How do they do these things? Are these athletes superhuman? Actually, your own body, after years of practice and training, might be able to do some of the same things.

All bodies are built to move. Your body and brain work together to set your legs and arms in motion. How does it all work? Let's start with a simple motion, like running.

What kinds of skills does it take to be a great soccer player or pole-vaulter?

Run, Don't Walk

What part of your body do you think of first when you think of running? Feet! When you run, each foot propels you off the ground—upward and forward. As you lift your foot, your ankle **joint** allows it to bend upward. Then you bring your leg forward and press your heel down against the ground. Your foot rolls forward. Then your other foot comes down and propels you forward. Now you're running!

People run for lots of reasons.
Why do you run?

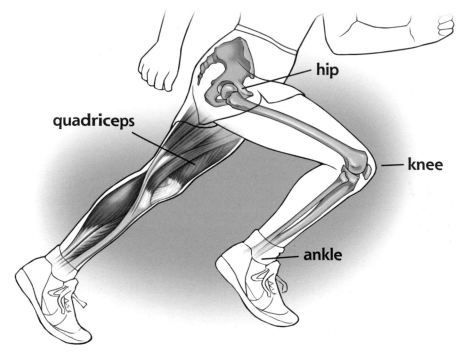

quadriceps

hip

knee

ankle

Each foot has 28 bones, 33 joints, and 19 muscles. The three main joints in your leg are your hips, your knees, and your ankles.

Getting a Leg Up

What do your legs have to do with running? A large muscle in your thigh, called the **quadriceps**, is what lifts your leg up, allowing you to run. The quadriceps muscle is attached to your thigh bone. Muscles move the bones they are attached to by tightening, or contracting. What other part of your body allows you to run?

Your legs and feet are made of many bones, muscles, and joints. All of them work together to help you move.

Long, strong leg bones help to hold you up. The muscles attached to your leg bones contract and allow you to move the bones. When your foot hits the ground, whether your leg is bent or straight, your knee joint also supports the weight of your body.

Artificial limbs attached to the knee joint allow these athletes to run.

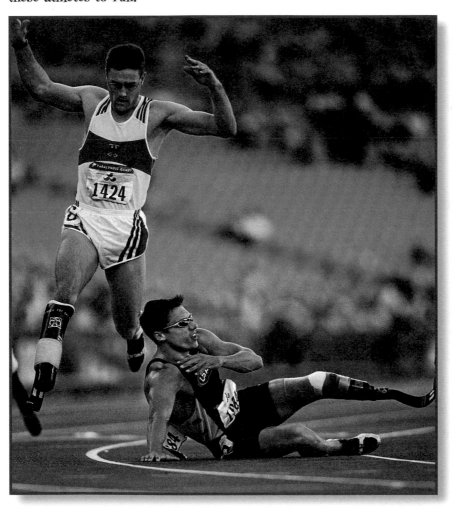

Why Do You Need Knees?

Your knees allow your legs to bend and move. Without your knee joint, running would be pretty awkward. Try to run without bending your knees—it's almost impossible!

The knee is a joint that connects the bones in your thighs to the bones in your calves. Just as the joints in your feet are some of the smallest in your body, the knee joint is actually the biggest. It works like a hinge, enabling your lower

As these teammates get ready to pass the baton in a relay race, they try to take as long a stride as possible without sacrificing speed.

leg to swing back and forth. You could almost compare your knee to a door hinge that lets the door swing open and shut.

The knee is put into action when your quadriceps muscle receives a message from your brain to contract. When the muscle contracts, it lifts your leg upward. As you lift your leg, your knee bends naturally. Now, you can swing your foot forward and begin to run.

Hitting Your Stride

The bones and muscles in your legs perform similar functions whether you are running or walking. There are some differences, however. When you walk, one foot will always be in contact with the ground. But when you run, there is a point in your stride when neither foot is touching the ground.

Watch Your Step

Years ago, a simple canvas shoe with a thin rubber sole, and therefore very little support, was all you could buy in the way of a running shoe. Today, workout shoes are much more high-tech. The top part of a shoe is made with lightweight, breathable fibers that keep your feet from getting too hot. The inner cushioning of the shoe is made of a very dense foam; some shoes even use a special kind of gel. The outer sole is usually made with a special kind of rubber. Today, almost all running shoes have structures inside the shoe that support the arch of the foot.

breathable fiber

outer sole

foam

gel

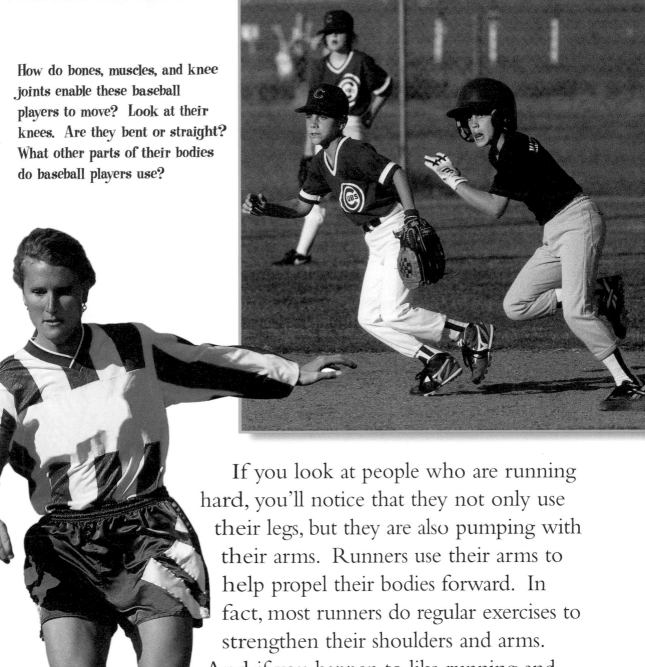

How do bones, muscles, and knee joints enable these baseball players to move? Look at their knees. Are they bent or straight? What other parts of their bodies do baseball players use?

If you look at people who are running hard, you'll notice that they not only use their legs, but they are also pumping with their arms. Runners use their arms to help propel their bodies forward. In fact, most runners do regular exercises to strengthen their shoulders and arms. And if you happen to like running and have strong, **flexible** arms, you may want to try another sport: basketball.

Slam Dunk

Take a look at a basketball game in progress. What do you see? Arms in constant motion—swinging back and forth, up and down, and bending and straightening. In fact, basketball players sometimes seem to be all arms as they block, pass, dribble, and shoot.

Professional basketball players have broad shoulders and strong arm muscles. A single muscle attaches the shoulder bone, or blade, to the upper-arm bones. When this muscle contracts, it enables the players to lift and move the bones in their arms. As players lift and throw the ball, their shoulder blades move up and down.

In the photo to the left, one player bends her elbows and gets ready to shoot the ball up into the basket while the other raises his arms to block her action. The player in the photo to the right lifts his arms above his head and . . . slam dunk! Would any of these actions be possible without flexible joints and strong arms and shoulders?

Your Shoulder Is a Holder

The shoulder blade itself actually forms a **socket** that "holds" your upper-arm bone. The shoulder is a unique joint that allows you to lift and move your arms forward, backward, and sideways. Held inside this socket, your upper arm bone can also **rotate** in almost a complete circle. Try it. Lift your hands in front of you way above your head. Then rotate your arms, and bring your hands back down behind you as far as you can.

All these movements are necessary for playing basketball. When you block other players, your shoulder joint allows you to lift your arms sideways and in front of the other players. When dribbling the ball, players often reach their arms back to move the ball forward quickly.

This player is reaching her arm back to dribble the ball. As she does this, her upper arm rotates in her shoulder socket.

The player with the ball is rotating his arm very far back in the shoulder socket. The other player lifts his arms sideways to block him.

Elbowing In

Your elbow is where your upper arm bone and forearm bones meet. But your elbow joint is more like your knee joint, though, than your shoulder joint. It acts like a hinge, allowing your lower arm to move in two directions—up and down—but not sideways or backward.

Your shoulder joint allows a large range of motion. Your elbow joint allows another, smaller range of motion. Combine these two ranges of motion and you can do some pretty amazing things with a basketball! For instance, you could reach behind you, quickly grab the ball from another player, lift your arms and the ball high into the air, bend your elbows back, take aim, then bend your elbows forward to shoot the ball into the basket.

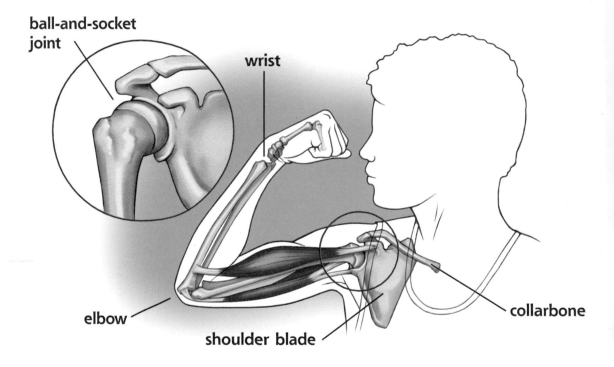

The top of your upper-arm bone is rounded, like a ball. It snaps into the curved part of the shoulder-blade socket, forming a joint. The shoulder-and-arm joint is a ball-and-socket joint. A single muscle connects the shoulder blade, the collarbone, and the upper arm. This muscle allows you to lift the arm at the shoulder.

This player flicks her wrists just as she releases the ball. This small motion controls the direction of the ball.

It's All in the Wrist

In basketball, this saying can be very true! The wrist acts like a hinge, allowing the hand to move up and down to dribble the ball. It allows you to position your hands in order to catch the ball or set it up for a free throw.

Your lower arm is actually made up of two bones. These bones meet at your wrist, forming your wrist joint. This joint allows you to turn your hand from a hands-down position to palms up.

The wrist itself is made of eight small bones. These bones form about 20 joints that allow you to make smaller, sideways motions. A slight twist of the wrist could send the ball off course or produce "nothing but net." Maybe it *is* all in the wrist!

A Sure Cure for Winter Boredom

During the winter of 1891, a New England teacher became frustrated when he could not keep students interested in his sports class. So he asked one of his colleagues, James Naismith, to invent a new indoor sport.

Using two peach baskets and a soccer ball, Naismith invented "Basket Ball." He attached the baskets to either end of the gym and told students that the goal was to throw the ball into the other team's basket. Each time the ball made it into the basket, the game would stop and someone would have to take the ball out.

Through the years, the designs for both the basket and the ball have been changed, but the original 13 rules that Naismith made for the game are actually still followed.

Tennis is another sport in which the player's arms and shoulders get a real workout.

Basketball and Beyond

Your arms allow you to do much more than dribble, pass, and throw. You may also spread your arms to help you to balance. They support your weight and lift your body into a push-up or a handstand. Your arms can also propel you forward as you swim, row a boat, or cartwheel across the floor. Now let's try a sport with a whole new twist: gymnastics.

Taking Flight

Leaping, flipping, and spinning, gymnasts seem to spend as little time as possible with their feet on the ground. It's often hard to tell just what part of their bodies they are using to perform each stunt. In fact, it almost seems as if magic is helping gymnasts to swing around the bars, propel themselves high above the ground, and twirl on a narrow balance beam.

Well, any gymnast could tell you that it's definitely not magic. Instead, the stunts they perform are a combination of tremendous strength, amazing flexibility, and perfect control —the result of long, grueling hours of practice and training. And, more than most other sports, gymnastics requires that you develop and learn to

Gymnasts demonstrate a variety of skills as they perform on the balance beam (left) or on the parallel bars (right).

control the muscles in your body—from the ones that point your toes to those that extend your pinkie finger.

Muscle Power

No gymnastics stunt is possible without muscle power. Male and female gymnasts must master different routines for competition. A female gymnast needs strong leg muscles to sprint to the springboard and punch off it, hurling her body up and over the horse. A male gymnast needs strong shoulder and arm muscles to perform on just about every piece of equipment, from the rings to the parallel bars to the pommel horse. Strong back and **abdominal muscles** are also needed for everything from handstands to walkovers to flips.

How is this gymnast using her abdominal and back muscles?

Gymnasts put all 640 skeletal muscles to use!

So, how do you make muscles stronger? The saying "use it or lose it" should give you a clue. The muscles you can "use," or control, in your body are called **skeletal muscles**. These muscles are attached to, and therefore help you to move, your bones.

U.S. Olympic star Dominique Dawes exhibits strength, flexibility, and balance as she holds a pose on the balance beam.

Put these muscles into regular use, and they will become stronger. But if you stop using them on a regular basis, your muscles will lose their strength.

Gymnasts increase the strength of their muscles by using them every day, often for many hours. In addition to practicing gymnastic stunts, gymnasts do hundreds of sit-ups, push-ups, and other strengthening exercises. Many gymnasts also use weight machines as part of their training.

Flex It

Having strong muscles is one requirement for gymnasts, but being able to do things like touching your toes to your head is another. So, gymnasts also spend long hours stretching their bodies to increase their flexibility. Flexibility is necessary for many stunts—just look at the pictures on these pages. Do you see any movements that *don't* require great flexibility?

Perhaps the most amazing example of gymnasts' flexibility is their ability to arch, bend, and twist their backs in so many ways. How is this possible? Well, the backbone or spine is actually not a single, long, solid bone. Instead, it is made up of 33 small bones, called **vertebrae**. These vertebrae are connected by **cartilage**, a tissue similar to bone, but softer and flexible. (Another part of your body that is made of cartilage is your nose.) This cartilage is what allows you to bend and twist the vertebrae that make up your spine.

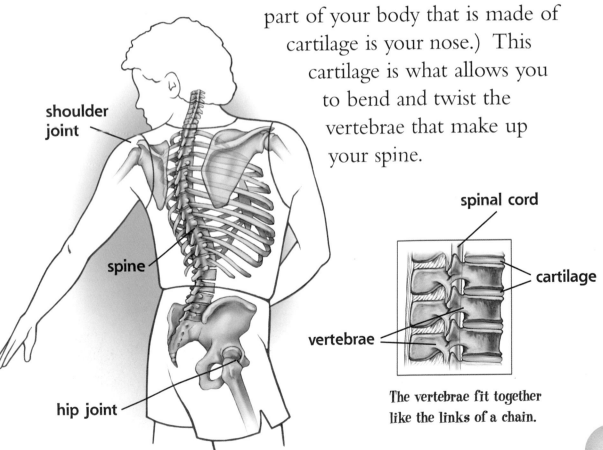

shoulder joint

spine

hip joint

spinal cord

cartilage

vertebrae

The vertebrae fit together like the links of a chain.

Brain Power

For a gymnast, mental concentration can be just as important as strength and flexibility.

Gymnasts learn to control each move through concentration and repetition. Then, once the body begins to recognize and remember certain moves, a gymnast is able to fine-tune the action. For example, once a gymnast learns to do a back walkover that leads into a back flip and lands in a split, he or she can then concentrate on extending the fingers and pointing the toes while performing the stunt.

Such perfect control doesn't start in your leg or arm muscles; it starts in the brain. The brain is

A Balancing Act: How to Do a Back Walkover

Start

connected to the muscles by the **spinal cord**. The spinal cord, which is surrounded and protected by the vertebrae, runs up your back and into your brain. Nerves attached to the spinal cord are connected to the muscles.

When you want to move, your brain sends a message along the nerves that run down through the spinal cord and into each and every muscle.

Practicing a series of movements over and over again also helps your brain, nerves, and muscles remember what to do. But even after many repetitions, athletes know that performing complicated moves still requires concentration! Take a look at any gymnast. No matter what stunt is being performed, you'll see a look of intense concentration on the gymnast's face.

Finish

Get Moving

Your brain is powerful. So are your bones and muscles, your joints and nerves. Together, they work to put your body in motion as you run, play basketball, or perform gymnastic stunts.

To be a top athlete in any sport requires dedication and years of training the body. Luckily, you don't need to be a top athlete simply to enjoy the pleasure of being in motion. The possibilities are endless, and your body is built to move.

What do you like to do? Run, hike, play basketball, swim, somersault? Hop on your bicycle, grab a ball or a bat, get on your swimsuit, or your running shoes. Put your body in motion!

Websites

To learn more about sports and how the body works, check out these Websites:

www.freezone.com/action

kidshealth.org/kid/

GLOSSARY

abdominal muscles: muscles in the front of the body below the ribs and above the hips

cartilage: a strong, elastic tissue that connects bones in humans and animals

flexible: able to bend

joint: a place where two bones meet, such as the knee, elbow, or shoulder

quadriceps: a large muscle attached to the thigh bone

rotate: to turn in a circle

skeletal muscle: muscle that is attached to bones and makes the bones move

socket: a hollow place in a bone where another bone fits in (forming a joint)

spinal column: a series of bones in your back that supports your body and protects the spinal cord

spinal cord: a thick bundle of nerves that begins in the brain and runs through the spinal column

vertebrae: the small bones that stack to make up the spinal column

INDEX